# Great
# Quotes
# from
# Great
# Teachers

Published in the United States by
Great Quotations Publishing Company
1967 Quincy Court
Glendale Heights, IL  60139

Printed in Hong Kong

*This book contains
the words of men and women
who have dedicated their lives
to educating others.
It is through their selfless example
that the next generation
will be prepared for the future.*

-*Christa McAuliffe*-
*The first teacher in space, Christa had intended to conduct lessons from the Challenger. The nation witnessed a great tragedy when the shuttle burst into flames.*

*I touch the future.
I teach.*

*-Christa McAuliffe*

*What are we doing
here? We're reaching for the stars.*

*-Christa McAuliffe*

*Our children must never lose their zeal for building a better world.*

-Mary McLeod Bethune

*There is a place in God's sun for the youth "farthest down" who has the vision, the determination, and the courage to reach it.*

-Mary McLeod Bethune

*All my life I have worked with youth. I have begged for them and fought for them and lived for them and in them. My story is their story.*

-Mary McLeod Bethune

*The whole world opened
to me when I learned to read.*

-Mary McLeod Bethune

*Invest in a human soul.
Who knows? It might be a
diamond in the rough.*

-Mary McLeod Bethune

*Faith is the first factor in a life devoted to service. Without faith, nothing is possible. With it, nothing is impossible.*

-Mary McLeod Bethune

$\mathcal{O}$ur goal is not so much
the imparting of knowledge as
the unveiling and developing of
spiritual energy.

-Maria Montessori

$\mathcal{T}$he child endures all
things.

-Maria Montessori

*-Maria Montessori-*
*Developed the Montessori Method:*
*Children learn through all their senses,*
*to develop a sense for order and logical*
*thought.*

*What is the greatest
sign of success for a teacher...?
It is to be able to say
"the children are now working as
if I did not exist."*

-Maria Montessori

*The first idea that the child must acquire, in order to be actively disciplined, is that of the difference between good and evil; and the task of the educator lies in seeing that the child does not confound good with immobility, and evil with activity...our aim is to discipline for activity, for work, for good; not immobility, not for passivity, not for obedience.*

-Maria Montessori

*We teachers can only
help the work going on,
as servants wait upon a master.*

-Maria Montessori

*If help and salvation
are to come, they can only come
from the children, for the
children are the makers of men.*

-Maria Montessori

*And if education is always to be conceived along the same antiquated lines of a mere transmission of knowledge, there is little to be hoped from it in the bettering of man's future. For what is the use of transmitting knowledge if the individual's total development lags behind?*

-Maria Montessori

*A new education from birth onward must be built up. Education must be reconstructed and based on the laws of nature and not on the preconceived notions and prejudices of adult society.*

-Maria Montessori

*And the directress must take great care not to offend the principles of liberty... not to make the child feel that he has made a mistake, for the materials will guide him in his error.*

-Maria Montessori

*And such is our duty toward the child: to give a ray of light and to go on our way.*

-Maria Montessori

*To stimulate life, leaving it then free to develop, to unfold, herein lies the first task of the educator.*

-Maria Montessori

*The greater or lesser efficiency of the child depends upon the teacher and how she presents the educational materials to the child. She must know how to render the material attractive to the child so that it will be most effective, although the degree of effectiveness can only be determined by the teacher herself and by her method of presentation.*

-Maria Montessori

*-Anne Sullivan-*
*A teacher of the blind and deaf, including*
*Helen Keller, Ms. Sullivan taught using the*
*manual alphabet and the Braille system.*

*I have thought about it a great deal, and the more I think the more certain I am that obedience is the gateway through which knowledge, yes, and love, too, enter the mind of the child.*

-Anne Sullivan

*My heart is singing for joy this morning. A miracle has happened! The light of understanding has shone upon my little pupil's mind, and behold, all things are changed.*

-Anne Sullivan

*I am beginning to suspect all elaborate and special systems of education. They seem to me to be built upon the supposition that every child is a kind of idiot who must be taught to think.*

-Anne Sullivan

*People seldom see the halting and painful steps by which the most insignificant success is achieved.*

-Anne Sullivan

*L*anguage grows out of life, out of its needs and experiences...Language and knowledge are indissolubly connected; they are interdependent. Good work in language presupposes and depends on a real knowledge of things.

-Anne Sullivan

*I never taught language for the PURPOSE of teaching it; but invariably used language as a medium for the communication of thought; thus the learning of language was coincident with the acquisition of knowledge.*

-Anne Sullivan

The child needs a framework within which to find himself; otherwise, he is an egg without a shell.

-Theresa Ross

*When someone is taught the joy of learning, it becomes a life-long process that never stops, a process that creates a logical individual. That is the challenge and joy of teaching.*

-Marva Collins

*I have proven that children labeled "unteachable" can learn.*

-Marva Collins

*- Marva Collins -*
*Ms. Collins is an respected educator and the founder of Westside Preparatory School in Chicago.*

*Determination and perseverance move the world; thinking that others will do it for you is a sure way to fail.*

-Marva Collins

*Before we even attempt to teach children, we want them to know each of them is unique and very special. We want them to like themselves, to want to achieve and care about themselves.*

-Marva Collins

*Education is painful and not gained with playing games or being average.*

-Marva Collins

*Excellence is not an act but a habit. The things you do the most are the things you will do best.*

-Marva Collins

*How many children are discouraged from pursuing an education because teachers have taken it upon themselves to judge who can achieve and who cannot? I wasn't there to judge my students. My job as a teacher was to get their talents working. And that's what I tried to do.*

-Marva Collins

*N*one of you has ever
failed. School may have failed
you. Goodbye to failure,
children. Welcome to success.

-Marva Collins

*A*n error means a
child needs help, not a
reprimand or ridicule for doing
something wrong.

-Marva Collins

*You were not born to fail. You were born to succeed. But you are going to have to learn. No one owes you a thing in this life. I don't want anyone to give you children anything-except your dignity.*

-Marva Collins

*Readers are leaders. Thinkers succeed.*

-Marva Collins

*I* got so tired of hearing those proverbs when I was a child. Now I use them all the time. Sometimes they are the best way to say what needs to be said. I teach them to my students. I have a collection of proverbs for class discussion and writing assignments.

-Marva Collins

*Trust yourself. Think for yourself. Act for yourself. Speak for yourself. Be yourself. Imitation is suicide.*

-Marva Collins

*There is a brilliant child locked inside every student.*

-Marva Collins

*Education is the key to unlock the golden door of freedom.*

-George Washington Carver

*I know of nothing more inspiring than that of making discoveries for ones self.*

-George Washington Carver

-George Washington Carver-
*Best known for his work with the peanut,*
*his constant quest for knowledge inspired*
*his students to reach their full potential.*

*I* love to think of nature
as an unlimited broadcasting
system through which God speaks
to us every hour if we only tune
in.

-George Washington Carver

*Y* ou can't teach people
anything. You can only draw
out.

-George Washington Carver

*Become a person who neither looks up to the rich or down on the poor...take your share of the world and let other people have theirs.*

-George Washington Carver

*H ow far you go in life depends on your being tender with the young, compassionate with the aged, sympathetic with the striving, and tolerant of the weak and the strong. Because someday in life you will have been all of these.*

-George Washington Carver

*Look about you, take hold of the things that are here. Let them talk to you, and you will learn to talk to them.*

-George Washington Carver

*I am interested in young people for they must catch the vision...we must set the creative to work.*

-George Washington Carver

*Stop talking so much. You never see a heavy thinker with his mouth open.*

-George Washington Carver

*Education is understanding relationships.*

-George Washington Carver

*Life requires thorough preparation. Veneer isn't worth anything.*

-George Washington Carver

*One of the things that has helped me as much as any other is not how long I am going to live, but how much I can do while living.*

-George Washington Carver

*-Albert Einstein-*
*This brilliant physicist developed the*
*theory of relativity, yet never forgot*
*about the effect of science on humanity.*

*The important thing is not to stop questioning.*

-Albert Einstein

*The process of scientific discovery is, in effect, a continual flight from wonder.*

-Albert Einstein

*The bitter and the sweet come from the outside, the hard from within, from one's own efforts.*

*–Albert Einstein*

*I never think of the future. It comes soon enough.*

*-Albert Einstein*

*I believe that a simple and unassuming  manner of life is best for everyone, best for both the body and the mind.*

-Albert Einstein

*Try not to become a man of success but rather try to become a man of value.*

-Albert Einstein

*Education must have an end in view, for it is not an end in itself.*

-Sybil Marshall

*If the majority culture know so little about us, it must be our problem, they seem to be telling us; the burden of teaching is on us.*

-Mitsuye Yamada

*Teaching, is not just a job. It is a human service, and it must be thought of as a mission.*

-Dr. Ralph Tyler

*The purpose of learning is growth, and our minds, unlike our bodies, can continue growing as we continue to live.*

-Mortimer Adler

*The marvelous thing about learning style is that every teacher can help to provide a warm prevailing breeze to lift all those "kites" and help them soar. Sometimes the strings may get tangled up, but now we can understand how a little more dimension and space can keep them free and flying.*

-Emilie Piper

*Freedom of inquiry, freedom of discussion, and freedom of teaching - without these a university cannot exist.*

-Robert Maynard Hutchins

*The university exists only to find and to communicate the truth.*

-Robert Maynard Hutchins

*I*t is possible for a
student to win twelve letters at a
university without his learning
how to write one.

-Robert Maynard Hutchins

*T*he object of education is
to prepare the young to educate
themselves throughout their lives.

-Robert Maynard Hutchins

*My idea of education is to unsettle the minds of the young and inflame their intellects.*

-Robert Maynard Hutchins

*All who have meditated on the art of governing mankind have been convinced that the fate of empires depends on the education of youth.*

*-Aristotle*

*When preparing a presentation for a class I look for surprises, I found that surprise, that juxtaposition. It's that creation of an expectation and then hitting you with cold water to make you wake up-that's what I feel the great life of art is all about. What I don't understand is why teachers let themselves collapse into boredom.*

-Steven Urkowitz

*I see the mind of the five-year-old as a volcano with two vents: destructiveness and creativeness.*

-Sylvia Ashton-Warner

*At the desk where I sit, I have learned one great truth. The answer for all our national problems-the answer for all the problems of the world-comes to a single word. That word is "education."*

-Lyndon B. Johnson

*The three R's of our
school system must be supported
by the three T's:
teachers who are superior,
techniques of instruction that
are modern,
and thinking about education
which places it first in all our
plans and hopes.*

*-Lyndon B. Johnson*

*We think of schools as places where youth learns, but our schools also need to learn.*

*-Lyndon B. Johnson*

*The combined opposition cannot prevent us from advancing so long as we have the road to books and schools open to us. Even the snub given to our political condition is as nothing compared with what it would be to shut the doors of the school against us.*

-Benjamin Lee

*We must open the doors of opportunity. But we must also equip our people to walk through those doors.*

-Lyndon B. Johnson

*I am a teacher.*
*A teacher is someone who leads.*
*There is no magic here.*
*I do not walk on water,*
*I do not part the sea.*
*I just love children.*

*-Marva Collins*